ART DECO
PAINTING AND
DESIGN

ART DECO PAINTING AND DESIGN

CHARTWELL
BOOKS, INC.

Published by Chartwell Books
A Division of Book Sales Inc.
114 Northfield Avenue
Edison, New Jersey 08837
USA

0-7858-1017-X

This book is produced by
Quantum Books Ltd
6 Blundell Street
London N7 9BH

Project Manager: Rebecca Kingsley
Project Editor: Judith Millidge
Designer: Wayne Humphries
Editor: Clare Haworth-Maden

The material in this publication previously appeared in
*Art Deco Source Book, Art Deco: An Illustrated Guide to
the Decorative Style, Encyclopedia of Art Deco, Art Deco:
An Illustrated Guide, 20s & 30s Style*

QUMDDPD
Set in Times
Reproduced in Singapore by United Graphic Ltd
Printed in Singapore by Star Standard Industries (Pte) Ltd

CONTENTS

THE
ART DECO
STYLE

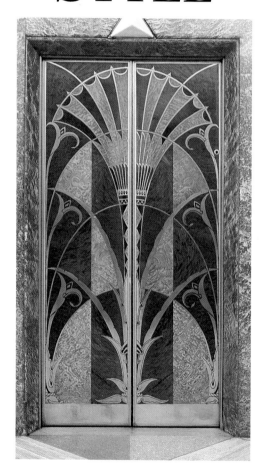

Art Deco is today regarded as a highly fertile chapter in the history of the applied arts. There is continuing debate, however, on the exact definition of the term "Art Deco" and the limits of the movement it encompasses. When the Art Deco revival first began, around thirty years ago, it was viewed as the very antithesis of Art Nouveau – indeed, the theory was that the new style was spawned in 1920 to eradicate its predecessor, which history had already judged a grave, but mercifully brief, transgression against good taste. Today this theory has been proved incorrect: Art Deco is not the opposite of Art Nouveau; it is in many aspects an extension of it, particularly with its pre-occupation with lavish ornamentation, fine materials, and superlative craftsmanship. Nor did it, as was previously believed, take root abruptly in 1920 and flower for a brief ten years until eclipsed by the economic collapse of the 1930s.

Although World War I has generally been taken as the dividing line between the Art Nouveau and the Art Deco epochs, in fact the latter was conceived during the transitional prewar years and, like its predecessor, it was an evolving style that neither began nor ended at any precise moment.

Right: This petite *commode by Paul Iribe, 1912, was one of the furnishings commissioned for the Jacques Doucet apartment.*

WORLD WAR I
Many items that are now accepted as pure Art Deco – such as furniture and *objets d'art* by Emile-Jacques Ruhlmann, Paul Iribe, Clément Rousseau, and Paul Follot – were designed before or during the outbreak of hostilities, and thus the movement cannot be rigidly defined within the decade 1920–30. Had it not been for the four-year hiatus created by World War I, in fact, the Art Deco style would probably have run its full and natural course by 1920.

It is hard to define the main characteristics

Opposite page: An elevator door from the Chrysler Building, New York, 1928–30, created by William van Alen.

L'Océanie

of Art Deco, because the style drew on such a host of diverse and often conflicting influences. Many of these came from the avant-garde painting styles of the early years of the century, so that elements from Cubism, Russian Constructivism, and Italian Futurism – abstraction, distortion, and simplification – are all evident in the Art Deco decorative arts vernacular. But this was not all: examination of the style's standard repertoire of motifs, such as stylized flower clusters, young maidens, geometry, and the ubiquitous *biche* (doe), reveals various influences from the world of high fashion, from Egyptology, the Orient, African tribalism, and Diaghilev's Ballets Russes. From 1925, the growing impact of the machine can be discerned in repeating or overlapping images, or later, during the 1930s, by streamlined forms derived from the principles of aerodynamics. All this resulted in a highly complex amalgam of artistic influences, defying description by one single phrase, though the term "Art Deco," derived from the Exposition des Arts Décoratifs et Industriels Modernes held in Paris in 1925, remains perhaps the most appropriate one.

A MODERN STYLE
The Art Deco style followed on immediately from Art Nouveau at the end of the nineteenth century. The latter had mostly relied on floral motifs to pattern and ornament its buildings and other artifacts, whereas Art Deco was thoroughly modern in turning away from the winding, sinuous qualities of Art Nouveau, looking instead to those of abstract design and color for color's sake; and when turning to

Left: "L'Oceanie" ("Oceania"), one of a series of exotic place images on a 1921 calender designed by George Barbier.

nature for inspiration, it preferred to portray animals, or the beauties of the female form. Where Art Nouveau had been heavy, complex, and crowded, Art Deco was clean and pure. The lines in Art Deco did not swirl around like the center of a whirlpool; if they curved, they were gradual and sweeping, following a fine arc; if they were straight, they were straight as a ruler. After Art Nouveau, with its intricate and elaborate floral patterns and intertwining vines, and Empire and Consulate furniture, the coming of Art Deco and the pure, no-nonsense simplicity of everyday objects must have filled their users with a sense of relief and clean, uncluttered well-being. If Art Deco design was bold, bright, and innocent, the reality of the age was far more sinister, far less comfortable and secure. Art Deco could be light-hearted on one level and deadly serious and practical on another. As the style in a time of unprecedented change, it was fluid enough to reflect that change.

THE ORIGINS OF ART DECO

The style evolved in France, notably in Paris, where it manifested itself emotionally, with exuberance, color, and playfulness. Elsewhere in Europe, and later in the U.S.A., it was given a more intellectual interpretation based on theories of functionalism and economy, and this element of design is known today as Modernism, to distinguish it from the high-style French variant, which is sometimes called "high Art Deco." Both, however, are aspects of a twentieth-century preoccupation with contemporary sources and inspiration, unlike the revivalism of prewar styles.

Right: An English enameled cigarette case dating from 1931, its design clearly influenced by the Ballets Russes.

Above: One of the premier ceramics designers in Art Deco France was René Buthaud, who created this stoneware vase after attending the 1931 Exposition Coloniale in Paris featuring African art.

Just as the Art Deco style had replaced Art Nouveau in France, so did Art Deco in turn yield to Modernism during the mid-1920s, its demise in fact beginning at its very moment of triumph, the International Exposition. The movement's first tenet – that form must follow function – remained unchallenged by any later schools of design, but its second, relating to decoration and craftsmanship, proved its undoing. By 1926, the loosely knit band of French Modernists – Francis Jourdain, Pierre Chareau, Le Corbusier, Robert Mallet-Stevens, and René Herbst – had become increasingly outspoken in its criticism of those Art Deco designers who catered to select clients by creating elaborately crafted *pièces uniques*, or limited editions.

THE MACHINE AGE

The Modernists argued that the new age required excellent design for everyone, and that quality and mass-production were not mutually exclusive. The future of the decorative arts, they believed, did not rest with the wealthy few and should not be formed by their esthetic preferences alone; an object's greatest beauty lay in its perfect adaptation to its usage. Each age must create a decorative style in its own image to meet its specific needs, and during the late 1920s this aim was best realized by industry's newest means of production: the machine. Existing concepts of beauty, based on the artisan and his hand tools, thus needed to be redefined to meet the dictates of the new machine age.

THE INFLUENCE OF MODERNISM

Modernism made rapid progress during the late 1920s, although most designers took a stance less severe than the functionalism that was espoused by its most ardent adherents.

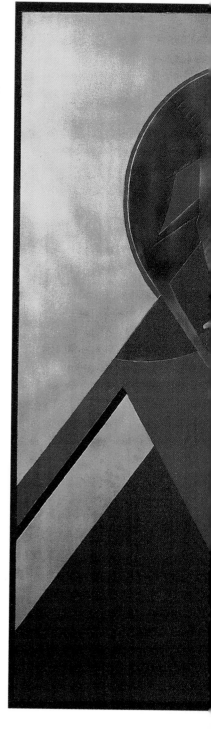

Right: Group of Dancers, *an elegant* moderne *ivory and bronze scupture by Paul Philippe.*

Below: The Metal Lady, *1923, by Russian sculptor Alexander Archipenko, whose work was defined by its abstract Cubism.*

As Paul Follot, a veteran designer, observed in 1928: "We know that the 'necessary' alone is not sufficient for man and that the superfluous is indispensable . . . or otherwise let us also suppress music, flowers, perfumes . . . and the smiles of ladies!" Follot's viewpoint was shared by most of his designer colleagues – even if logic called for the immediate elimination of all ornamentation, humankind was not psychologically prepared for such an abrupt dislocation in lifestyle. Most designers thus opted for a middle ground, creating machine-made items that retained an element of decoration – which, ironically, had often to be hand finished.

EARLY FUNCTIONALISM

Outside France, functionalism had a longer history, having dominated much decorative-arts ideology since the end of the Victorian era. In Munich, the formation of the Deutscher Werkbund in 1907 carried forward the logic and geometry at the heart of the Vienna Seccession and Glasgow movements some years earlier. In contrast to both the French Art Nouveau repertoire of flowers and maidens, and Germany's own lingering *Jugendstil*, the Werkbund placed emphasis on those functional designs that could be mass-produced. A reconciliation between art and industry, updated to accommodate the technological advances of the new century, was thus implemented, with ornament given only secondary status.

THE BAUHAUS

These ideals were realized more fully with the formation of the Bauhaus in Germany, which in turn inspired the Modernist strain that took root in American decorative arts during the late 1920s. After World War I, many European and Scandinavian designers followed the German example by creating

Left: The Hoover Factory in London, 1933, designed by Wallis, Gilbert, and Partners, incorporates Egyptian and other favored Art Deco motifs.

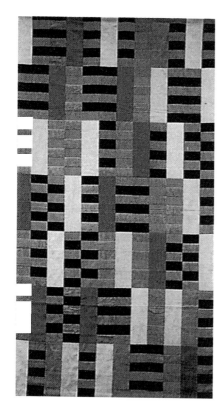

Above: This carpet, Arc-en-Ciel (Rainbow), was produced by Lucien-Boux, c.1926, to a geometrical design by the French architect and interior decorator Eric Bagge.

Right: The dramatically illuminated spire of the Chrysler Building, 1928–30, lights up the New York night sky.

Bauhaus-inspired furnishings and objects. Indeed, examination of contemporary European art reviews shows that ornament was sparingly applied outside France and, although a certain amount was tolerated, the high-style embellishments of Paris between 1910 and 1925 were viewed by artists of other nations as a Gallic eccentricity which should not be permitted outside French borders.

The high style's only real success abroad was in American architecture, where it was adopted to enhance America's new buildings, particularly skyscrapers and movie palaces. The U.S.A. lacked a modern style of its own during the early 1920s, so its architects looked to Paris for inspiration and leadership in art as they always had in the past.

ART DECO'S WIDE-RANGING INFLUENCE

The paintings and graphics of the interwar years are difficult to place in an Art Deco context. Many brilliant artists whose work falls beyond the proper scope of this book, such as Léger, Matisse, Vlaminck, and van Dongen, at times incorporated motifs in Art Deco style into their works on canvas and paper. Others, such as Rouault, Dérain, Marcoussis, and Braque, utilized a similar range of identifiable Art Deco motifs only when venturing into the field of the applied arts to design textiles and rugs.

ARTISTIC CROSSFERTILISATION

The boundaries between those who qualify as Art Deco exponents and those who do not are therefore far from finite. Most artists used a range of avant-garde mannerisms to solve traditional problems of design and composition. Some of these – for example, abstraction by means of Cubism and elongation, or the Fauves' preoccupation with bright colors –

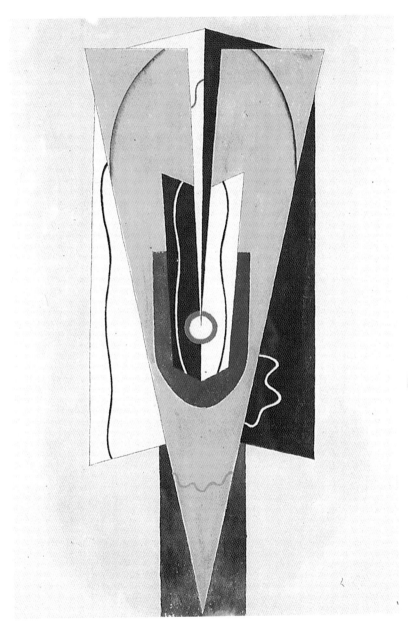

Above: A carpet designed for Jacques Doucet by Louis Marcoussis, c.1926. The Polish-born Marcoussis was also a noted printmaker.

Left: Better known for his Cubist sculpture, the Hungarian-born Joseph Csaky created Abstraction *in 1908.*

Right: British ceramics designer Clarice Cliff created this charming musical duo as part of her Age of Jazz *series of cutout, painted figures.*

were used by almost every Modernist artist. A study of painters who are considered today to fall within the Art Deco movement reveals certain common denominators by which an individual artist can be judged.

DEFINING ART DECO ARTISTS

Firstly, most Art Deco graphic artists were not innovative – they drew their inspiration from themes introduced by other Modernist artists, or schools of artists, often during the early years of the century, which they developed for their own purposes. Another criterion is that Art Deco graphics are decorative, designed to fit into the furniture ensembles of the era. Jean Dupas, for example, created paintings in a style which conformed to that of the furnishings in the room in which they would hang. They were, in the final analysis, decorative rather than artistic compositions. The same interpretation can be applied to the period's book illustrations and posters, many of which contained images found on contemporary ceramics, glassware, and sculpture.

Yet it is the mixing of all these influences that made Art Deco the style it is. In the hands of genius, the objects transcended their sources. In the hands of competent designers, or plagiarists, they might become drab or garish, but they were, nevertheless, truly Art Deco.

ART DECO PAINTING

Preceding page: Aldo Severi's untitled oil painting illustrates Art Deco's preoccupation with the decorative elegance of the female and animal forms.

Right: Montmartre, 1925, an oil on board work by Jean Lambert-Rucki.

Below: This figure by Japanese-born artist Tsuguharu Foujita combines an Oriental technique with a Western subject.

Painting during the Art Deco period had tremendous variety: it could be decorative or avant-garde, sleekly streamlined or lushly ornamented, highly representational or markedly abstract. Not all works of art painted during the 1920s and 1930s can, of course, be termed Art Deco, since the term is generally applied to design and not to fine art. Indeed, there is really no such thing as specifically Art Deco painting. It is possible to talk of Cubism, Surrealism, and Expressionism as coherent styles, but Art Deco painting never really existed in any convincing way. Strictly speaking, Art Deco derived its name from the Exposition des Arts Décoratifs et Industriels, which did not have a painting pavilion. Although the distance between the decorative arts and fine art as not as great as many people think, the best painting of the 1920s and 1930s certainly had little to do with the Art Deco style.

What does still exist, however, are examples of work by particular individuals that describe, or record in some way, the spirit of Art Deco, and some artists' works, whether because of their use of color or geometric techniques, their stylization or, more frequently, their inclusion in contemporary interior decoration or architecture, are nevertheless considered outstanding examples of the genre.

Art historians looking back at the art between the wars find examples of the best in the work of Picasso, Matisse, and the Surrealists. There is really very little question that artists of the stature of Picasso, Mondrian, Kandinsky, and others pushed forward the limits of painting, enriching the visual language beyond a stale academicism. Although these artists are now seen as the giants of twentieth-century art, it would be wrong to disregard the contributions of less well-known artists who communicated their message more readily, and also illustrated the taste of the age. Between the two extremes there is no contest on the grounds of quality, but minor art is often a more accurate indicator of public taste than the works of geniuses ahead of their time.

ART AND GRAHIC DESIGN

Within the lexicon of 1920s' and 1930s' style, some of the most powerfully conveyed sets of images are held within the interlinked worlds of art and graphic design. Posters, illustrations, and works of art have become interwoven with the style of these two decades, to the extent that one image is able to evoke a whole range of associations concerning the twenty years in question. It would be almost impossible to pin this phenomenon down to one set of reasons. Nevertheless, it is partially because of the extraordinary way in which, during this rich, highly creative period, various disciplines crossfertilized each other and grew together. Architects would design typefaces, painters would design houses, graphic artists would create costumes, poster designers would be influenced by architects, and so on. Therefore, while divisions between disciplines were still maintained, with artists essentially remaining artists and architects remaining architects, there was a distinct shift in the way in which practitioners within the various fields saw

Left: This exotic urban landscape is a 1926 design for a backcloth by Russian artist Natalia Gontcharova for the Ballets Russes production danced to Stravinsky's Oiseau de Feu (Firebird).

Above: A Modernist students' apartment block designed by Walter Gropius, 1925, illustrates the Bauhaus style.

themselves and applied their talents.

The prevalent atmosphere, that artists and designers were breaking new ground for a new age, meant that opportunities for experiments in different fields came into being more readily than had previously been known.

THE SPIRIT OF THE AGE

Form and meaning within design in general shared motifs derived from a common interest in the redefinition of artistic and design parameters. It was as if a new language had been invented by an avant-garde which keyed into the modern obsessions with the machine and rationality and cut across the conventional boundaries between areas of design, art, and theory. This was coupled with a feeling for the indeterminable, yet recurrent idea of the "spirit of the age."

There were certain events which facilitated the growth of this creative mélange. The setting up of the Bauhaus was one such event. The school was founded in 1919 in Weimar, Germany, now under the new regime of the socialist president Friedrich Ebert, and under the direction of Walter Gropius. It was not so much the thrust of the early Bauhaus teaching, with its attempt to wed art and craft, that makes it important in this context. More importantly, the school provided a focus for the artistic, creative, and intellectual life of post-World War I Germany, which lasted for 14 brief years. At times the school acted as a clearing house for many of the foremost artists and designers in Europe. Indeed, several artists, painters, designers, and architects considered prime movers in the world of design between the wars found their way to, and through, the Bauhaus. Paul Klee, Wassily Kandinsky, László Moholy-Nagy, Marcel Breuer, and Mies van der Rohe are but a few.

Right: A reproduction by Cassina of the original Red and Blue Chair *of 1917 by de Stijl architect-craftsman Gerrit Rietveld.*

Below: Composition with Red, Yellow and Blue, 1937–42, by de Stijl artist Piet Mondrian.

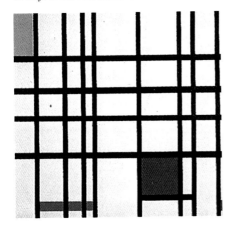

Definite links were forged between the Bauhaus in Germany and the de Stijl movement in The Netherlands, led by Theo van Doesburg and Piet Mondrian, and the *Vhutkemas* (art schools) in Russia, whose teachers included Kasimir Malevich, Vladimir Tatlin, and El Lissitzky. This further added to the ferment of design theory and practice in Europe at this time. By the mid-1930s the *Vhutkemas*, the Bauhaus, and the de Stijl movement had all met their demise. The rises of Stalin and Hitler put paid to the avant-garde tendencies of the institutions and movements in central and eastern Europe. These eventualities forced designers and artists to travel, and many set their sights on the New World,

making their way to England as a matter of course and leaving their marks, by way of influence and design and later by practice, in the United States.

CROSSING THE DISCIPLINES

This crossdisciplinary influence, which is so characteristic of the interwar years in Europe, can be seen in many instances. In 1920 Paris the Purist movement, led by Le Corbusier and Amadée Ozenfant, determined to produce art which employed the painting as a "machine for the transmission of sentiment." The magazine *L'Esprit Nouveau* was published at this time (from 1920 to 1925) and formed the basis of Le Corbusier's seminal 1923 book,

Vers une Architecture which contained the similar idea that the house "is a machine for living." Fernand Léger, too, professed to be influenced by the machine age, and the subjects within his paintings took on the appearance of machined, cylindrical surfaces, far removed from artistic devices which had come before in his work.

DE STIJL

In The Netherlands, the founders of the de Stijl movement also produced an eponymous journal to give vent to their own feelings about art, architecture, and the world in general. The paintings of Piet Mondrian can be seen as the gradual rationalization of perception and

representation into the horizontal, the vertical, primary colors and black, white, and grays. Formally speaking, these ideas broadly tie in with the Modernist movement's esthetic and can be found expressed to their fullest in Rietveld's 1925 Schröder House in Utrecht. Not an architect but a designer, Gerrit Rietveld built the house as a challenging exercise in three-dimensional planar composition, in much the same way that he had rendered his famous *Red and Blue Chair* in 1917, with color picking out the structural detail.

THE RUSSIAN STYLE

El Lissitzky, the Russian Constructivist artist who had been traveling in Europe during the 1920s, published an article on Rietveld upon his return to Russia in 1925, so aiding the spread and knowledge of European avant-garde ideas in art, architecture and design among the students and intelligentsia of yet another country. In Russia itself, the Constructivist movement had its own particular artistic language, adopted as the official revolutionary art. For those Europeans attuned to the thoughts behind Constructivism, it represented a reduction and rejection of traditional artistic representation and was wedded in purpose to social change and a strong belief in "the machine." Consequently, the power of industry – once in the hands of the workers – for bringing about change in the social order was the ultimate Utopian message. After 1921, when Constructivism was abandoned as the official revolutionary art form and the New Economic Policy was brought into action in the U.S.S.R., the artists behind

Left: Tango, *casein on canvas by Erica Giovanna Klein. This image combines Cubist and Futurist influences.*

the movement found that their ideas had no outlet. However, people like Moholy-Nagy, who had links with the Constructivists and who were later to become influential in imparting artistic theory and practice to their pupils at the Bauhaus, made sure that the principles of Constructivism were not allowed to die. Rather, they saw them subsumed into the general vocabulary of artistic usage.

ANTIORNAMENTATION

Traces of the influence of the Constructivist idea are apparent in many images readily associated with European design during the 1920s. The fact that Constructivism, de Stijl, and later Bauhaus ideas were expressed in a strongly geometric formal language only serves to heighten the sense that during the 1920s at least, the abandonment of unnecessary ornament in avant-garde, but obviously not *all* modern design, came to be seen as a powerful sign system. This in turn was seen to underline the existence of a common ground shared by forward-thinking designers working in all disciplines.

The formal language adopted by the avant-garde in Europe at this time cannot be viewed in isolation from the rest of the world of art. Indeed, the boundaries of what was possible and what was acceptable in terms of visual representation were opening up every day. The artistic language developed by Braque and Picasso had been realized relatively early in terms of the Art Deco period. Cubism, as a recognizable artistic style, existed by about 1915, but between the years 1920 and 1928

Right: La Naissance d'Aphrodite, *an oil on canvas painting by Paul Véra dating from 1925, depicted the birth of Venus in a Cubist manner.*

Right: Josephine Baker, *lacquer on wood, c.1926, by Jean Dunand.*

Picasso was still producing large Cubist still lifes like *Three Musicians* (1921) and *Three Dancers* (1925), which were, by then, very much a part of acknowledged art practice and therefore existed to be drawn from as part of a formal language.

The history books almost totally ignore the work of Tamara de Lempicka – surely the most representative of the period's portrait painters – the murals of Jean Dupas, the portraits of Kees van Dongen, or the later works of Raoul Dufy, reproducing instead the abstract innovations of Paul Klee, Pablo Picasso's classic nudes of immediately after World War I, or the rigidly thoughtout and constructed canvases of Piet Mondrian. This actually misrepresents the prevailing taste of the period. The artists commanding the highest prices at auction in Paris between the wars were Maurice Utrillo and Maurice Vlaminck. In retrospect, we can see that the host of canvases they produced then were just watered-down versions of their early work, but that was what the public wanted. There is no use in being highbrow or snobbish about the decorative arts of the period – for even artists as great as Picasso were willing to turn their hands to stage design, pottery, and furniture.

What is perhaps curious about the paintings that reflected the taste of the period most accurately was that they were almost always figurative, and in particular there are a great number of portraits that, even if we dismiss them as vulgar and modish, give a clear insight into the characters and tastes of their sitters. The large number of portraits or figure studies in the Art Deco style were really just illustrations of the period. Although there was generally little place for abstraction in Art Deco-style painting, there were some exceptions to the rule.

THE SIMULTANIST STYLE

Robert Delaunay and his wife Sonia had been deeply involved with the most advanced art in Paris since before World War I. Quickly adopting the lessons of Cubism from Picasso, Braque, Juan Gris, and Fernand Léger, Robert Delaunay produced paintings of Paris – the Eiffel Tower, Saint-Severin Church – and such motifs of the modern world as the airplane and the motor car. By the time of the outbreak of the war, he had distilled his art into pure abstraction, where fields of intense color collided with one another. Developing a style that was called "Orphism," Robert Delaunay's work provided inspiration for Art Deco design. The sweeping, circular curves and fields of intense color could be adapted to almost any other medium. It was his wife, however, who really developed and used the possibilities of the Simultanist style, as it was also known, to the full. Photos of Sonia Delaunay-Terk at the 1925 Exposition show her in Simultanist dress sitting on a car painted in the house colors. Her designs were all the rage, becoming *the* look for the sophisticated and avant-garde culture vulture. Bright and pleasing to the eye, her style brought a refreshing change after the heavy, exotic palette made popular by Bakst and Erté's costume designs for the Ballets Russes. The cut was also far more practical, severe, and modern.

FERNAND LÉGER

Another painter who is still regarded as important, and who could be said to reflect Art Deco preoccupations, was Fernand Léger.

Above: The Russian-born Sonia Delaunay produced this watercolor, which she called Simultané (Simultaneous). *The colorful fabric design is typical of the artist's bold, geometric output.*

Left: Le Corbusier designed the Pavillon de L'Esprit Nouveau for the Paris Exposition of 1925. Its modernity caused a scandal among the organizers.

Right: An elaborate gouache and ink drawing by Jean Dupas, 1928.

A friend and ally of Le Corbusier and Amadée Ozenfant, his pictures hung in the Pavillon de l'Esprit Nouveau at the 1925 Exposition. If Le Corbusier's architectural preferences were to provide houses that were machines for living in, Léger painted large murals and canvases that reflected the age's obsession with machinery. His canvases are peopled with robotlike figures painted in the brightest of color combinations. What he aimed to do was to personalize the machine and employ it as subject matter, an attitude that ran throughout Art Deco in its more Modernist vein.

MATISSE AND DUFY

The painters Henri Matisse and Raoul Dufy also contributed to the Art Deco influence. Matisse's interest in exotic subject matter, inspired by his visits to Morocco, reflected the contemporary French obsession with the colonies. Oriental art had been in vogue since the mid-nineteenth-century, but Matisse's exquisite sense of decoration reinstilled it with a vigorous, modern feel. Dufy, who had failed to win a commission for a large mural for the swimming-pool of the *Normandie*, produced painting after painting of the Côte d'Azur and Marseilles and its sailors at the same time as the south of France became the playground for the rich.

The many faceted nature of Jean Dupas's talent was also applied to painting. In Emile-Jacques Ruhlmann's pavilion, *Hotel d'un Collectionneur*, at the 1925 Exposition, Dupas displayed a large mural entitled *Les Perruches ("The Parakeets")*, a theme that was equally dear to Matisse. Dupas's many murals and screens for the *Normandie* and other private commissions, although executed in lacquer among other media, were in essence large paintings. Exotic and rich in subject matter, they were fine examples of the decorative tendencies of painting in the Art Deco style.

Tamara de Lempicka was probably the most typically "Art Deco" of all the portrait painters, whose whirlwind social life and distinctive portraits reflected the glittering aspect of the era and style. Born Tamara Gorska to a prosperous Polish family near Warsaw, she married a Russian, Thadeus Lempitzski (Lempicki), while in her teens. The couple arrived in Paris toward the end of World War I. Deserted by her husband during the 1920s, de Lempicka decided to support herself and her daughter Kisette by painting. She enrolled at the Académie Ransom, where she studied with Maurice Denis, a disciple of Cézanne,

Below: Dawn, *a gessoed-wood, 32-panel wall decoration for the Grand Salon of the ocean liner* Normandie *by Jean Dunand and Jean Dupas, c.1933-34.*

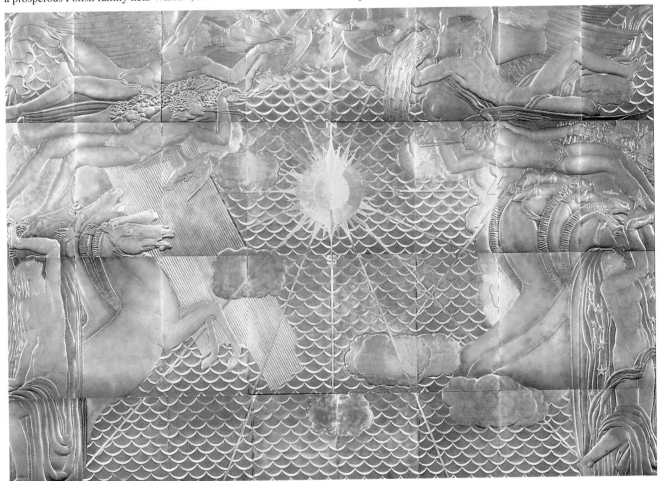

Above: Portrait of Arlette Boucard, *1928,*
by Tamara de Lempicka. It is a sensuous
depiction of the daughter of a scientist who
had invented the medicine Bacteol (written
on the prow of a ship in the background).

as well as André Lhote, the theoretician of
Cubism. Thereafter she painted the portraits
of other eastern European refugees (mostly
of royal lineage), famous writers, successful
businessmen, fellow artists, and her family.
Her dramatic, vividly hued portraits were often
sensuous and suggestive, sometimes surreal
or frightening. Especially memorable are those
with strong backgrounds, be they architectural
or floral settings, or billowy folds of fabric,
or a line of ships' prows.

SENSUALITY AND SUGGESTION
In the view of some, de Lempicka's portraits
of women, now in vogue again, are garishly
hideous studies in eroticism. The Folies

Bergères, Ziegfeld's Follies, and Josephine
Baker dancing in the nude are all highly suggestive and informative portraits of the risqué
fast set that Nancy Cunard was part of. Semi-
clad nudes provoke the viewer with pointed
breasts behind thin layers of diaphanous silk,
or thin coverings of black Spanish lace. Like
Foujita's sitters, or the hermaphrodite little girls
in Balthus paintings, de Lempicka's sitters look
at the spectator with a coy, languorous gaze.
Between 1924 and 1939 she painted about a
hundred portraits and nudes; these were
dramatically composed works, usually boldly colored (but sometimes black and white),
highly stylized and charged with energy,
sensuality, and sophistication. Partly angled

Cubism, partly fashion illustration, they were positive expressions of the Art Deco style and should therefore have given her an accordingly classic reputation. Other painters of this sort of genre were Otto Dix and Christian Schad, who did for Berlin what de Lempicka had done for Paris, but rather better. Arguably, their work has been more enduring, too.

MARIE LAURENÁIN

In sharp contrast to de Lempicka's handsome, somewhat aggressive works, were the ethereal paintings of Marie Laurenáin, which are often characterized as highly feminine because of their pastel hues, female subjects and innate "prettiness." They were nevertheless strong, distinctive images, and they appeared prominently within contemporary interiors, including those of her brother-in-law, André Groult. This versatile artist also designed rugs and carpets, as well as creating stage sets and costumes for the Ballets Russes' production of Francis Poulenc's *Les Biches*.

RAPHAEL DELORME

Female figures dominated Art Deco canvases, and nowhere more boldly than in the paintings of Bordeaux-trained Raphael Delorme, whose bulky, muscular nudes were often situated in bizarre architectural settings, wearing incongruous headdresses or surrounded by fully dressed maidservants, and mixed neo-classical and modernist images in a strange but appealing two-dimensional style. Indeed, an entire group of Bordeaux painters emerged during the Art Deco period, including not only Delorme, but also Jean Dupas, Robert Pougheon, André Lhote, René Buthaud, and Jean Despujols. Although their monumental and allegorical paintings of women tended toward the neo-classical, they were

Above: Flamant Rose (Pink Flamingo), *an oil on card painting by Raphael Delorme. The vase-bearing woman is seen amid a variety of Cubist motifs, with the title subject open-winged behind her.*

Above: A faience vase by the versatile artist René Buthard, 1925, featuring a monumental female figure typical of the Bordeaux painters' genre.

Above right: A verre églomisé panel by René Buthard, 1925 depicting a neo-classical, flower-draped nude.

wholly of the period in terms of drawing and colors, as well as in such specific details as stylized flowers, makeup, hairstyles, and costumes. Dupas, in particular, developed a highly distinctive and abstract style which captured precisely in its elongation and dehumanizing expressions the general mood of the period.

Pougheon studied at the Ecole des Beaux-Arts in Bordeaux and then at that in Paris, where he developed an abstract style in which the subject's anatomy was given an angular muscularity of often heroic proportions. Some of his works are quintessentially Art Deco in their extreme stylization, while others portray allegorical figures in naturalistic settings. Domergue painted portraits of Parisian socialites, theater celebrities and nudes, in an engaging style in which certain facial features were exaggerated. Buthaud, like Dupas, switched media with great facility. His paintings, often rendered initially as cartoons for his stained-glass windows, or *verre églomisé* panels, incorporate all the softness and sensuality of his designs for ceramics. André Lhote was self-taught, and achieved landscapes, genre scenes, and figural works which were somehow less caricatured and rather more starkly geometrical and spiritual than the works of the other painters.

ANIMALIERS

Some French artists during the 1920s adopted a Modernist style in portraying animals. The premier *animalier* painters were Paul Jouve, Jacques Nam, and André Margat, and they chose to treat their subjects in isolation, often silhouetted against a white ground. Felines – leopards and panthers in particular – and snakes and elephants were popular, all painted in slightly abrupt or faceted brush strokes to reveal the beast or reptile's innate power and rhythm. Jouve was the most diverse, generating a large body of *animalier* etchings, drawings, watercolors, woodcuts, and oils. He frequently worked with artists in other fields, such as Jean Dunand for murals on the ocean liner *L'Atlantique*, and with the bookbinder Georges Cretté to design plaques for his book covers.

One of the most popular Art Deco artists, especially in the United States, was the French-born Louis Icart, whose colored lithographs, etchings, and aquatints perfectly captured the image of the chic, attractive, sometimes slightly risqué woman of the 1930s, part Hollywood poster girl, part Parisian fashion plate. Typically, she reclined in a gossamer gown, her soft hair was usually Marceled, her high-arched brows pencil thin, her eyes heavily shadowed and her lips perfectly reddened Cupid's bows. She was often smoking (a cigarette holder was almost obligatory) and was accompanied by an elegant dog, usually a greyhound, poodle or Borzoi.

Left: Fumée (Smoke), *a drypoint etching by Louis Icart, 1926. Icart specialized in painting women in erotic poses.*

Right: A perspective of the Rockefeller Center in New York executed in pencil, paste, and gouache on board by John Weinrich in c.1931.

Below: Pearls, and Things and Palm Beach (The Breakers) by Emil J. Bisttram, a Hungarian emigré to the U.S.A. who worked in advertising and also painted moderne *images.*

THE AMERICAN STYLE

Austrian, Scandinavian, and American painters also created works that can loosely be termed Art Deco, especially their stylized portraits of chic or androgynous women. The Paris-based American painter Romaine Brooks, for example, depicted Una, Lady Troubridge, in a dapper man's suit and with short hair, complete with monocle and a pair of dachshunds, while the Danish-born Gerda Wegener painted sensuous female nudes in erotic poses, but in distinctly modern settings. However, although such American artists as Stuart Davis, Georgia O'Keeffe, Rockwell Kent, and Joseph Stella produced works in the machine-age idiom, celebrating industry, progress, and big-city architecture, the vigorous Art Deco painting that thrived in France did not on the whole influence American artists, except perhaps in the occasional allegorical mural that embellished a movie-theater lobby.

ART OR KITSCH?

In conclusion, although it is interesting and anecdotal, no true Art Deco-style painting is ever great art, it is rather more an example of entertaining camp.

Art Deco
Poster Design

The basic stylization – that is the geometricization – of the Art Deco period lent itself well to graphics of all kinds, including poster, book, and magazine illustrations, advertisements, packaging, and the like, which, whether mass-produced giveaways, or else limited-edition works of art, proliferated during the 1920s and 1930s. It is in poster design, where there is no question of high or low art, that an Art Deco style could truly be said to exist. During the 1920s, commercial art became a bona fide profession which, in turn, gave birth to the graphic artist. Graphic artists of the caliber of Rockwell Kent and Cassandre could employ all the devices of Art Deco design without needing to feel guilty. Their success relied directly upon their ability to reach the largest audience, to produce a popular image. Abstract art, which had taught so many designers the advantage of using clear form and strong, bold design, was not itself strengthened by Art Deco. It was, rather, watered down and made acceptable in its application to consumer items.

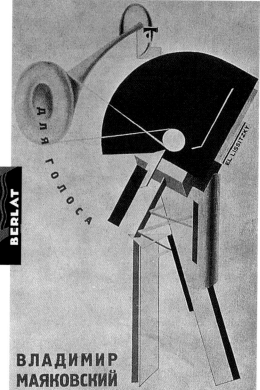

Preceding page: A poster by Wilquin advertising the Normandie *liner.*

Above: This French label for a chocolate bar is awash with Art Deco motifs and utilizes a typical typeface.

Right: For the Voice, a strong Constructivist image by the Russian artist El Lissitzky.

A particularly strong distillation of current visual languages between the wars can be found in the work of the poster designers in Europe, England and, to a lesser extent, the United States. The history of poster design really began during the late nineteenth century.

THE HISTORY OF THE POSTER
Early posters had been used to illustrate the ambitions and aspirations of political parties or, on a more intimate scale, limited-edition prints by Rowlandson, Gillray, and Honoré Daumier had provided a forum for the acid and biting criticism of the hypocrisies of the establishment. By the end of the nineteenth century, artists like Steinlein, Henri de Toulouse-Lautrec, Aubrey Beardsley, and Edward Penfield were producing works that truly understood the limitations and advantages of the poster medium. From them, other graphic artists learned the skills of successful poster design, as well as its role within twentieth-century society.

TECHNICAL PROGRESS
Printing methods, especially color reproduction processes, had vastly improved

Electrically tempered
BLUE GILLETTE
SLOTTED BLADES
shave better because
their cutting edge
- is harder
- is stronger
- is keener
- lasts longer

LARGE PACKET 2/6 · SMALL PACKET 1/3

Left: A Blue Gillette advertisement dating from 1937. Strong sans-serif imagery had found its way into advertising by the 1930s.

during the nineteenth and early twentieth centuries, as had the overall quality of the finished product, encouraging top-ranking artists and illustrators to accept commissions. Graphics had become bolder, broader, more geometric, less ornamented, and, perhaps most importantly, highly legible. The first of the century's sans-serif typefaces, "Railway," was designed in 1918 by Edward Johnston for the London Underground system.

NEW TYPEFACES

The Bauhaus typographer Herbert Bayer's "Universal" typeface, introduced in 1925, was void not only of serifs and other decorative elements, but even of capital letters. Even the Cyrillic alphabet took on strongly angular lines during the 1920s, in graphics by, among others, Vladimir Tatlin, El Lissitzky and Natalia Goncharova. In 1920s' France, however, decorative touches were added to – rather than subtracted from – typefaces, a logical development considering the vogue for decoration in every other medium. This was manifested primarily in the juxtaposition of thick and thin elements within a single letter, or in decorative shading that entirely eliminated a part of a letter. M. F. Benton's *Parisian* (1928) is a good example of thick-thin characters, while Cassandre's *Bifur* (1929) consisted of letters that were nearly unrecognizable, except for their gray areas.

Until the advent of commercial radio after World War II, the poster campaign was by far the most effective way of reaching a mass audience and informing it of the product on offer. Of course, the realization that, in a world

Right: A poster for Imperial Airways, 1930s. Travel advertisements celebrated the beauty of the machine as much as the exotic destinations promoted.

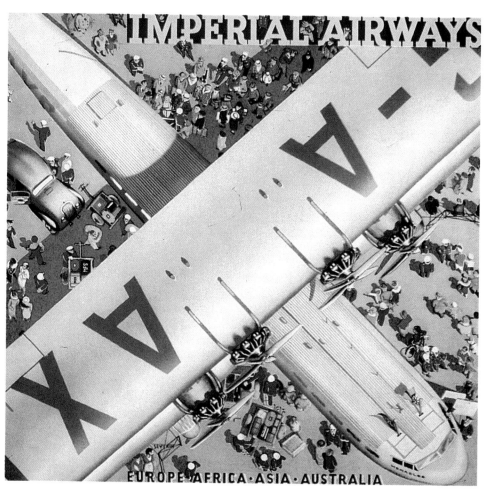

dominated by the poster, new posters had to be simple and powerful just to get their message across must have had an impact on the way in which the poster was conceived. That there was a large and varied "scrapbook" of visual ideas available to the poster artists to draw upon, in the guise of avant-garde art and architecture, was only to their benefit.

Posters had to be cheap to mass-produce, striking in design and arresting enough to catch the viewers' attention for long enough to tempt them to read the accompanying text. This latter attribute was not even essential, as the poster could work on the same level as a medieval stained-glass window, educating and informing an illiterate audience and

suggesting to them what they might like to acquire. Although the message was more mundane and down to earth than that of the medieval craftsmen, the result in terms of beauty was not necessarily less. The best and most memorable posters were equal to, if not better than, much so-called "fine art," and this was especially the case with Art Deco.

THE GROWTH OF ADVERTISING

The Art Deco poster was the first full-blown example of a sophisticated understanding of the advantages and idiosyncrasies of the world of advertising. This was hardly surprising, as the growth of the advertising industry and the medium of poster design were inseparable. Art Deco, the style of the consumer age, was applied with great success to the promotion of all the new consumer items, including the gramophone (phonograph), radio set, motor car (automobile), airplane, ocean-going liner, cosmetics, household appliances, and, of course, the Hollywood movies.

DYNAMIC SUBJECTS

The motifs of many of the vividly colored posters and graphics of the period were characterized by sheer energy and exuberance, in part the result of the new obsession with speed and travel that accompanied the fancy motor cars, fast trains, and elegant ocean liners which were so much an expression of the 1920s and 1930s. The one lasting theme and motif that ran throughout Art Deco posters and illustrations was that of the modish, self-possessed, and highly energetic woman. She would be the role model that any woman bent on self-improvement would have to emulate. Ever changing, she inspired people to part with their money in order to keep up with her. Unlike the idealized nudes and nymphs that peopled Art Deco sculptures, the women in posters were modern in every sense of the word. The sketches of Ernest Deutsch Dryden are a superb contemporary record. Women in the latest fashions stand with their companions around a Bugatti motor car ready to step in and set off – to where? Deauville, Cannes, Long Island, or a weekend party at a country house?

Above: a poster-type caricature of the French performer Maurice Chevalier, who first achieved fame in Paris revues of the 1920s. Note the sans-serif typeface.

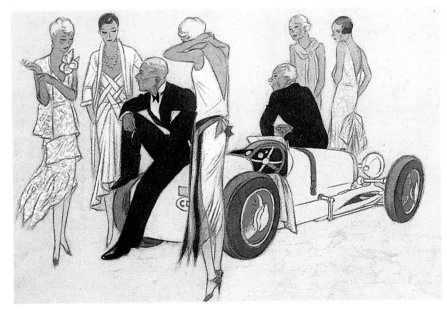

Left: Ernest Deutsch Dryden's pencil and gouache image of fashionably dressed people grouped round a Bugatti motor car.

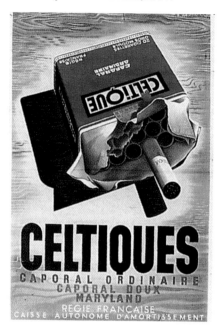

Dramatic, colorful and enduring, Art Deco posters can be divided broadly into two categories: theatrical and commercial (including travel and special events such as sports meetings, concerts, and art exhibitions). In Germany and Italy, the poster also became a dynamic (and extremely effective) propaganda tool for the Fascist regimes.

A. M. CASSANDRE

Perhaps the greatest poster designer and typographer of Art Deco Paris was the Russian-born Adolphe Jean-Marie Mouron, better known by his pseudonym Cassandre. Certainly his work is regarded as being among the most evocative of the period, and it was

arguably the most successful of his time. His distinctive graphic style – bright colors combined with subtle shading, bold lettering often juxtaposed with wispy characters, and strong and angular, flat images – won him numerous awards. Between 1923 and 1936 Cassandre used the poster as no one had before him. In his hands it represented an interface between the visual languages of the avant-garde and the ordinary public. The adept use of the pictogram, bold typeface, and skillful lithography meant that a combination of the elements of Constructivism, Cubism, and Modernist typeface design came together as a commercial tool and, many critics would say, a work of art.

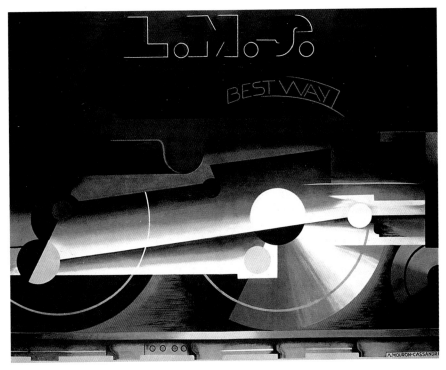

Left: A. M. Cassandre's lithographic poster for McCorquodale & Co., London, a British railway company.

Below: The dramatic bow of an unnamed French ship looms overhead in A. M. Cassandre's 1935 poster.

IMAGES OF TRAVEL

Cassandre was a self-confessed lover of architecture and hated "deforming details"; it is no accident, therefore, that some of his most enduring images were produced to advertise railways and shipping lines. After all, these posters were to represent the very machines which inspired the architects, which in turn inspired the artist. Thus, his poster *Nord Express* (1927), in which a streamlined, angled locomotive puffs decoratively, and his most famous single work, the fiercely frontal view of the ship for his poster for the liner *Normandie* (1935), represent the opposite ends of Cassandre at his most precise. In *Normandie,* the prow of the ship pushes forward out of the picture, as the majestic giant dwarfs the small tug beneath it. The stark outlines of the design and the stylized realism of the picture suggest to the viewer the qualities that the *Normandie* certainly had: including strength and elegance. In such posters, his work most reflected and utilized the current modern machine-esthetic-inspired visual language. As representations of distilled 1920s' and 1930s' style, they are hard to better.

PAUL COLIN

Cassandre was not the only poster artist operating in Paris. Indeed, when this period in Paris is discussed, it is often in terms of the three "C."s: Cassandre, Colin, and Carlu. Paul

Colin – whose often light-hearted illustrative style, although neither as austere nor as classy as Cassandre's, was equally effective – designed posters to advertise the visiting jazz luminaries at the Folies Bergère and other venues. Originally the poster artist and stage designer for the Théâtre des Champs-Elysées, he is perhaps most famous for his poster for "La Revue Nègre" of 1925, the show which introduced Josephine Baker to Paris, in which a saucy Josephine Baker is memorably depicted with two black jazz musicians.

"THE JAZZ STYLE"

It is with posters like these that the Art Deco style came closest to gaining the name "the jazz style." Deriving loosely from Cubist painting with its disjointed sense of perspective, the colors were jazzed up, as unlikely combinations of electric blue were juxtaposed with reds and livid greens. The overall effect was initially jarring, but then resolved itself into an energetic and fully comprehensible pictorial logic. Colin's posters were in a style rather reminiscent of that of Marc Chagall, the artist who had been the art commissar of Vitebsk in Russia in 1919. Colin took a similar route, moving away from figurative representation to a more geometric style which was inspired by Constructivism, consisting of overlapping planar surfaces. This style is particularly in evidence in his work for the Wiener and Docet Piano Company. Before this, Colin designed a series of posters to advertise Josephine Baker's recordings, as well as depicting Miss Baker in several paintings. He also designed stunning posters advertising not only other

Left: A 1925 poster by Paul Colin advertising the "Black Revue." This is perhaps his most famous work.

Above: Robert Bonfils's poster advertising the 1925 Paris Exposition Internationale des Arts Décoratifs et Industriels Modernes.

Left: This 1925 poster of Casino de Paris performer Mistinguett was created by Charles Gesmar.

Above: René Buthard's 1931 poster for the Société des Artistes Décorateurs.

performers, but cigarettes and other products, most of which featured human figures, sometimes highly stylized, sometimes lovingly caricatured in recognizable detail.

JEAN CARLU

The third "C.", Jean Carlu, can also be seen as a representative of the verve, vitality, and adaptability of creative people in Paris at this time, untrammeled by the idea that one discipline was enough. Carlu trained as an architect but, after losing an arm in an accident, gave up architecture and moved on to poster design. His output was of a similar standard to Cassandre and Colin's, but gravitated toward less glamourous goods, *Mon Savon* soap of 1927 and consequent advertisements for toothpaste probably being among his most successful executions.

Another artist operating in Paris at the same time, designing both posters and packaging, was Pierre Fix Masseau, whose Cassandresque style in the French Railway's *Exactitude* poster of 1932 served to underline the effectiveness and popularity of this style. Charles Gesmar, who is best remembered for his posters of the Casino de Paris performer Mistinguett, designed in a curvilinear and ornate style, *á la* 1900. He usually employed stark lettering, but occasionally became rather fanciful, with his letters resembling those of Jean-Gabriel Domergue on his posters for the dancers Maarcya and Gunsett.

Three memorable posters were created for the 1925 Paris Exposition by Charles Loupot, Robert Bonfils, and Girard. Loupot's designs cleverly juxtaposed industry and decoration, depicting a massive factory with wisps of black smoke cutting across clouds shaped like stylized flowers. Bonfils's image was by contrast totally decorative, featuring a stylized Greek maiden carrying a basket of flowers, accompanied by a dark, leaping deer.

RENÉ VINCENT

Another notable poster designer, René Vincent, forsook his architectural studies at the Ecole des Beaux-Arts in Paris for a career in the graphic arts and, to a lesser degree, ceramics. An illustrator for *La Vie Parisienne, The Saturday Evening Post,* and *L'Illustration,* Vincent also designed posters for the giant Parisian department store Au Bon Marché. His compositions often featured fashionable demoiselles playing golf, or bearing parasols, done in a crisp illustrative style that was heightened by contrasting blocked colors.

OCCASIONAL POSTER DESIGNERS

Many other French graphic artists provided the world of poster art with intermittent works. Jean Dupas, for example, turned his hand to a series of delightful advertisements for Saks Fifth Avenue, Arnold Constable, and others, with a facility that shows his great versatility. René Buthaud transposed the maidens on his stoneware vessels onto paper, some to herald the annual Paris salons. The identity of the prolific artist Orsi, whose name appears on more than a thousand posters, including images of Josephine Baker at the Théâtre de L'Etoile, remains an enigma. From the world of fashion, Gorges Lepape and Natalia Goncharova created posters in a predictably colorful and theatrical style which depicted Paris as the pleasure capital of the world.

In Britain, the United States, and Germany, most poster designs were pared down and geometric, using the bold, rectilinear typefaces

Right: Joost Schmidt's poster for the Bauhaus "Art and Technology" show, 1923.

that were fast becoming the norm. Among the primary exponents of the art of the poster in Britain was Edward McKnight Kauffer, an expatriate American who settled in London in 1914 (and returned to the U.S.A. in 1940). His poster design in *Flight* (1916) is different from these transportation images: a highly stylized representation of a flock of birds, it was inspired by a Japanese print as well as marked by the influence of the Vorticist movement, which flared briefly during World War I in London. It appeared in *Colour* magazine, which devoted one page per month to a poster design. This design was later taken up to advertise a national newspaper in 1919. Kauffer thought of himself as a painter until 1921, the year in which his work as a poster designer took off and he was able to

Right: A colorful and decidedly moderne *poster for London Transport by C. Paine, 1918.*

Far right: This stunning poster for Fritz Lang's Metropolis, *1926, betrays a German Expressionist influence in its graphics and the inspiration of New York in the cityscape.*

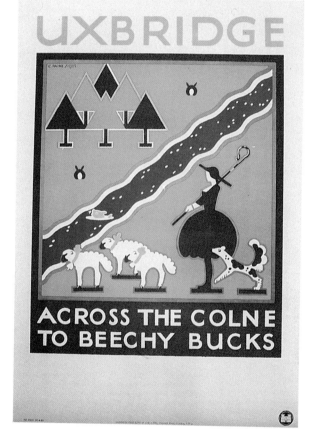

Left: Edward McKnight Kauffer's poster for Shell Petroleum, 1932.

Below: René Magritte's sheet-music cover for Le Tango des Aveux, *1925.*

consolidate his position. Prior to this, Kauffer had worked for Frank Pick, head of publicity on the Underground Electric Railway Company of London, producing posters of Watford, Reigate, and other rural places accessible by means of London Transport. These posters depended on a relatively simple, but stylized, representation of a landscape to suggest the idea of day-tripping to nearby ideal spot. While his London Transport posters tended to be quite Cubist and abstract, those of other designers were more colorful and representational, but always with easy-to-read typefaces. The French artist Jean Dupas, for example, designed a poster for London Transport showing a scene of elegantly dressed ladies in Hyde Park.

KAUFFER'S SIGNIFICANCE
By the mid-1920s Kauffer had consolidated his position in Britain as a leading poster designer; indeed, in 1925 there was a retrospective exhibition of his work featuring 56 of his designs, of which among perhaps the most famous today is his poster for Fritz Lang's masterpiece *Metropolis* and also for Shell Petroleum. After this point, Kauffer's work expanded to meet the influence coming from the continent, taking on board the motifs which are today so readily associated with this era. Kauffer also pioneered photomontage techniques, collaborating on several occasions with the celebrated photographer Man Ray. He further illustrated the tendency for designers to work in more than one medium by his designs for rugs (his wife, Marion Dorn, was a celebrated rug designer) and his collaboration with architect Wells Coates on the wall mural at Embassy Court, Coates's seaside apartment block in Brighton (1935).

BELGIAN AND DUTCH DESIGNERS

In Belgium, the Swiss-born Léo Marfurt formed a fifty-year-old association with the tobacco company van der Elst, for which he designed advertisements, packaging, and posters. In 1927 he formed his own studio, Les Créations Publicitaires, where he produced two world-class masterpieces of travel-poster art: the *Flying Scotsman* (1928) and *Ostende-Douvres* (around 1928). The former emerged as one of the most recognizable, enduring, and popular images of the interwar years. René Magritte, a magazine and advertising illustrator before he turned to Surrealism, also created some vibrant Art Deco poster images during the mid-1920s, while two other Low Country artists, Willem Frederik ten Brock and Kees van der Laan, produced posters for Dutch shipping lines.

SWISS AND GERMAN DESIGNERS

In Switzerland, Otto Baumberger, Herbert Matter, and Otto Morach designed for the fashionable men's clothing store, P.K.Z., as did the German Ludwig Hohlwein. Baumberger, trained as a lithographer and posterist in Munich, London, and Paris, worked principally in Zurich, where he helped to establish the Swiss School of Graphic Design. Matter is known principally for his pioneership of the photomontage technique in travel posters such as *Winterferien* (1934) and *All Roads Lead To Switzerland* (1935). Ludwig Hohlwein was Germany's most popular and prolific poster artist. His preference for virile, masculine images with which to advertise coffee, cigarettes, and beer later won him many commissions for Nazi propaganda posters.

Left: An advertisement for the P.K.Z. men's clothing-store chain, 1923.

Above: A Lucien Bernhard poster, 1929.

Left: A detail of the publicity poster for the movie The Shape of Things to Come, *1936.*

THE PARISIAN INFLUENCE

Hohlwein's real gift lay in his use of color in unexpected combinations. Other German posterists, such as Walter Schackenberg and Josef Fennacker, embraced a softer, more French-inspired style in their designs for theater and ballet performances.

The Hungarian Marcel Vertès established himself immediately after World War I as a leading poster artist in Vienna. He moved in 1925 to Paris where, apart from the publication of two volumes of lithographs, *Maisons* and *Dancing*, and occasional work for Elsa Schiaparelli, he lapsed into obscurity. His Viennese posters, however, were colorful and distinctly Parisian in their light mood.

Brilliant interpretations of the Art Deco poster were produced in other countries, but with less frequency, by Marcello Dudovich and Marcello Nizzoli in Italy; Maciej Nowichi and Stanislawa Sandecka in Poland; and Kauffer, Alexander Alexeieff, J. S. Anderson, and Greiwirth in Britain.

In some ways the poster, and design in general, across the Atlantic was to be deeply affected by the arrival of artistic and design talent from Europe. As the Nazis became more and more powerful, Europe became an increasingly difficult place in which to exist, and many artists emigrated.

DESIGN IN THE UNITED STATES

The list of names that finally found their way to the United States reads like a design hall of fame for Europe. The Austrian-born Lucien Bernhard, for example, had studied at the Munich Academy, from which he emerged as a versatile artist-architect, designing buildings, furnishings, and graphic works. In 1923 he emigrated to the United States, where in 1929 he cofounded the Contempora Group in New York. His poster style appears labored and undirected, but he was invariably treated with respect by contemporary critics.

LESTER BEALL

As far as home-grown American talent was concerned, the field was dominated by Lester Beall, a self-taught graphic artist whose clever use of photomontage and Modernist typefaces helped to promote, among other

things, the Works Progress Administration (W.P.A.) which was part of President Roosevelt's popular "New Deal" from 1935.

By this time Beall was surrounded by European talent: Cassandre, Mondrian, Carlu, the artists Max Ernst and Marcel Duchamp, Bauhaus teachers Gropius, Herbert Bayer, Breuer, and Moholy-Nagy, and photographers Man Ray and Cartier-Bresson.

EUROPEANS IN THE UNITED STATES
Clearly, at this time in the United States the thrust for innovative graphic design was

coming from Europe. Even famous American graphic icons, such as Raymond Loewy's bold design for the Lucky Strike cigarette pack in 1940, owe a great deal to the influence of Bauhaus-inspired sans-serif graphics. And the official posters for the 1939 New York World's Fair, depicting the quintessentially American image of the Trylon and Perisphere, came from the pen and airbrush of an expatriate Austrian, Joseph Binder. He, too, drew inspiration from the popular "scrapbook" of Modernist and avant-garde images which formed the basis of 1920s' and 1930s' style

in the graphic arts. The work of Vladimir V. Brobritsky, another highly talented immigrant, likewise captured the vibrant, alluring mood of interwar Paris.

Above: A poster produced to publicize Charlie Chaplin's movie Modern Times, *1936.*

48

Art Deco
Bookbinding
and Illustration

Right: A four-panel screen by Jean Dunand, featuring a trio of monkeys amid tropical vegetation. Dunand used similar motifs and techniques in bookbinding.

Below: Pierre Bonoit's Mademoiselle de la Ferté, *1926, binder Pierre Legrain, illustrations by Yves Alix.*

Preceding page: A rare and lavishly bound copy of Charles I. Philippe's book Bubu de Montparnasse, *designed by Paul Bonet.*

One of the most exciting areas of graphic Art Deco design was the book jacket, as well as the binding that encased the book. Indeed, the craft of bookbinding underwent a renaissance after World War I, although most observers were unaware that it had in earlier times attained a high degree of artisanship.

By long tradition, books in France had been published with flimsy paper covers, making them acceptable to the serious collectors who employed bookbinders to design and create covers for their favorite volumes. This system prevailed right up to the earliest years of the twentieth century. The binding's function was to preserve the text, and it was not considered as a means of artistic expression until the emergence of the Art Deco movement. At that point, however, the principles of artistic excellence together with excellence in craftsmanship caused a radical change. During the 1920s Paris was filled with small

presses, but as well as these there was still a strong tradition of wealthy people, like Huysmans's hero des Esseintes in *Against Nature*, who had their favorite books specially bound.

BOOKBINDING
Although book design may seem in some ways superfluous to the actual purpose of a book, no one who has held a fine-tooled, Morocco-leather binding in the hand, and turned the pages of handmade paper, can deny the sensual delights of sight, touch, smell and the pleasures of good design and craftsmanship that

such a book can give. A particularly fine example was the collaboration on the book *Bubu du Montparnasse* in 1929 by Charles I. Phillipe. The binding, designed by Paul Bonet, was accompanied by illustrations by the artist Dunoyer de Segonzac.

PIERRE LEGRAIN

Pierre Legrain, a noted furniture designer, must be credited with revolutionizing the art. In 1912, when Jacques Doucet disposed of his collection of antique furniture at auction, he presented his correspondingly important library of eighteenth-century books to the city of Paris, retaining only his collection of works by contemporary authors. The young Legrain, who had been more or less unemployed since his former employer Paul Iribe set sail for the United States in 1914, was retained to design the bindings in a modern style. Without prior experience, and largely self-taught, Legrain undertook the task in the *atelier* of the binder

Below: An opulent 1936 leather binding by J. K. van West covers Maurice Barrè's book La Mort de Venise.

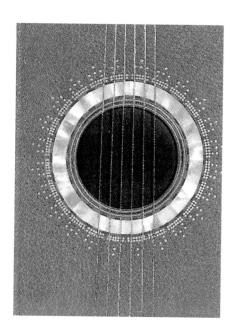

Above: A stamped and foiled Morocco-leather book binding for Colette's Chéri *designed by Rose Adler in 1925.*

Above right: François Coppée's Le Passant, *bound by Georges Adenis.*

René Kieffer. Doucet was at once impressed and commissioned more bindings. In a two-year period Legrain designed some 365 bindings for Doucet, all of which were executed by professional binders. By the early 1920s, Legrain's abilities had drawn the attention of other collectors, such as Baron Robert de Rothschild, Henri de Monbrison, and Baron Gourgaud, all of whom became regular and valuable clients. Legrain introduced an unusual and endearing selling ploy, donating to the patron the tools used on each binding.

THE AVANT-GARDE IN BOOKBINDING

Legrain's ignorance of traditional binding techniques served him well, for it allowed him to make free use of his creativity and to introduce materials not used before. From the start, his designs were avant-garde, in keeping with the revolution in design taking place throughout the decorative arts in Paris. In place of the lightly ornamented floral bindings of the prewar years, he introduced geometrical patterns in the same precious materials being employed at the time by Modernist *ébénistes* such as Emile-Jacques Ruhlmann, Clément Rousseau, and Adolphe Chanaux.

Indeed, some of the top names in French design applied their talents to book covers and sometimes used the same opulent materials as in their furniture and other designs.

BINDING MATERIALS

By the 1920s, bookbinding had become an extension of the Art Deco cabinetmaking craft, as exotic veneers and skins were borrowed in search of a means to modernize the age-old craft. Most Art Deco bookbinders incorporated bright colors, geometric elements, and sumptuous materials into their work. Hides such as snakeskin, *galuchat* (sharkskin), or vellum were interchanged with binding's traditional Moroccan leather. Decorative accents were provided in innumerable ways. For instance, the binding could be inlaid with a mosaic of colored leather sections, or with gold, silver, platinum, or palladium fillets, or it could be gilt-tooled, blind-stamped, or painted.

DECORATIVE PLAQUES

Further embellishment was provided by the application of decorative plaques in sculptured or veneered wood, lacquered silver or gold, enameled porcelain, bas-relief bronze, or carved ivory. The encrustation of mother of pearl, tortoiseshell, or semiprecious stones provided further esthetic possibilities. Exotic works were covered with Japanese prints or silk-mounted on cardboard. A matching slipcase completed the package for unique works. Although most of the premier Art Deco

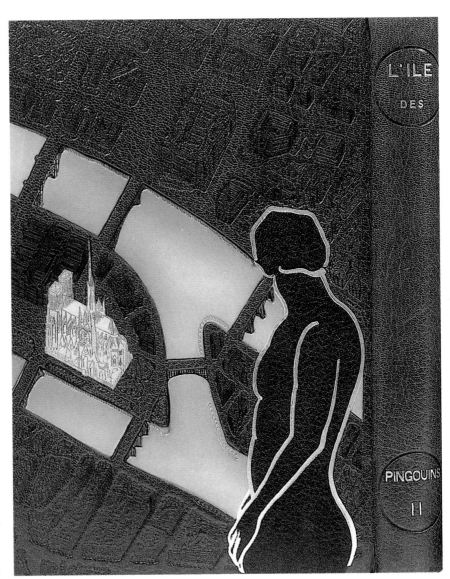

Above: L'Ile des Pingouins, *by Anatole France, 1926, bound by Henri Creuzevault.*

Right: A menu designed by the versatile François-Louis Schmied in 1926 for his friend Jean Dunand.

Below: Histoire Charmante de l'Adolescent Sucré. *The medallion was designed by François-Louis Schmied and executed by Jean Dunand; the binding is by Léon Gruel.*

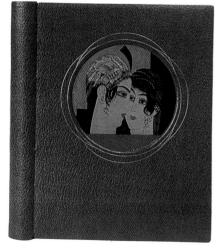

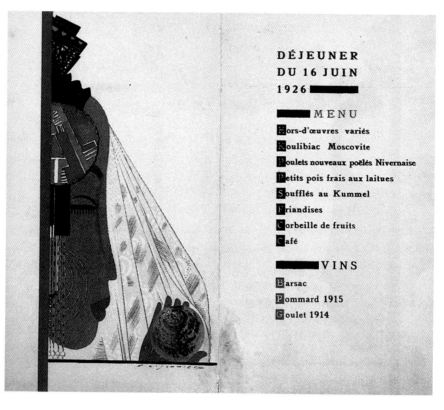

DÉJEUNER
DU 16 JUIN
1926 ▬

▬ MENU
Hors-d'œuvres variés
Koulibiac Moscovite
Poulets nouveaux poêlés Nivernaise
Petits pois frais aux laitues
Soufflés au Kummel
Friandises
Corbeille de fruits
Café

▬ VINS
Barsac
Pommard 1915
Goulet 1914

bookbindings included no letters on their covers, some incorporated the titles effectively, using gilt *moderne* letters to complement the prevailing geometric motifs.

MOTIFS AND SUBJECTS

The 1920s' binder drew mostly on the same repertoire of motifs used in other media. Combinations of lines, dots, overlapping circles, and centripetal or radiating bands were used to create symmetrical or asymmetrical compositions. The influence of the machine and new technology became increasingly felt toward 1930, particularly by Paul Bonet, who

emerged as Legrain's successor. The preferred motifs of the Paris salon during the early 1920s (such as the stylized floral bouquet or gazelle) quickly yielded to a fiercely geometric vocabulary found especially in such works as Creuzevault's *La Seine de Bercy au Point-du-Jour,* Legrain's *Les Chansons des Bilitis,* Kieffer's *Trois Eglises* and Bonet's *Les Poilus.*

As well as Legrain, Paris was home to a host of premier binders who worked in the Modernist idiom, including Georges Cretté (the successor to Marius Michel), René Kieffer, Jean Dunand, Paul Bonet, François-Louis Schmied, Louis Creuzevault, Georges Canape,

Far left: Maurice de Noisay's Tableau des Courses, *1921, a book bound by Charles Benoit and illustrated by J. L. Boussingault.*

Left: La Creation, *elegantly bound by François-Louis Schmied (who also provided the illustrations) in collaboration with Conin et Cie.*

and Robert Bonfils. Foremost among these was another Doucet protégée, Rose Adler, whose bindings for Doucet were even more exotic than Legrain's, and were sometimes encrusted with precious stones. Her maroon Morocco-leather binding for Colette's *Chéri* (1925) is stylish, with 12 metallic circles at the left giving way to a huge hemisphere at the right, which is actually the letter "C." enclosing the last four letters of the title.

ROBERT BONFILS

Legrain rarely designed figural bindings, but others, notably Bonfils, did – usually sharp-angled or modishly decorative silhouettes, seldom full-color figures. Bonfils was himself also an executor of bindings, working with André Jeanne, a professional binder who produced designs for Rose Adler and for

Left: J. C. Mardrus's Ruth et Booz, *1930, bound and illustrated by François-Louis Schmied; lacquered panel designed by Jean Dunand.*

such other gifted practitioners as Paul Bonet and the father-and-son team of Louis and Henri Creuzevault. Louis Creuzevault created abstract or floral patterns, as well as covers with three-dimensional applications of differently colored leathers. In 1930 he produced a binding for Georges Duhamel's *Scènes de la vie future* that was distinctly *moderne*.

ARTISTIC COLLABORATIONS

Many of these binders collaborated on commissions with artist-designers, and even with other binders. Schmied, in particular, was extremely versatile, participating in commissions as a binder, artist, or artisan with Cretté and Canape. The *animalier* artist Paul Jouves and the sculptor Guino contributed designs for ivory and bronze panels. Jean Dunand was likewise very active, creating lacquered and *coquille d'oeuf* plaques, and even wooden ones inlaid with detailed marquetry designs, for Schmied and other binders. His plaques were sometimes designed by Schmied, and included colorful landscapes, stylized floral motifs, abstract patterns, and exotic figures and animals. One handsome example was a striking roundel illustrating a panther and a young man for Rudyard Kipling's *Jungle Book*, or *Le Livre de la Jungle*.

FRANÇOIS-LOUIS SCHMIED

François-Louis Schmied, a man of many talents, not only designed covers but illustrated books; designed both them and their typefaces; created their lettering; made wood engravings of illustrations for them; and even printed them on his own presses. His bindings ranged from

Left: An English book cover created by American-born designer Edward McKnight Kauffer, who also designed carpets.

subdued monochromatic enlivened only by gilt lettering to opulently multicolored, often set with lacquer panels, usually executed either by Dunand or else by the Cubist-influenced designer Jean Goulden. A lovely Schmied binding for Paul Fort's *Les Ballades françaises* featured a green and silvered-metal plaque by Dunand showing stylized birds on a background of dots in a rainbow pattern.

PAUL BONET

Paul Bonet, a fashion designer turned bookbinder, was imaginative and innovative, using metallic bindings; cutout bindings that revealed a design on the endpapers; and other related but varying designs and lettering on the spines of works of more than one volume, such as on Marcel Proust's classic *A la Recherche du temps perdu*.

Some binders also incorporated photographic elements in their covers, among them Laure Albin Guillot, who specialized in microphotography, enlarging tiny biological specimens – such as plankton – to produce unusual, pseudoabstract designs. Many of her other bindings included human images, such as an erotic, back-posed nude on Pierre Loüy's *Les Chansons de Bilitis*.

LESSER BOOKBINDERS

Less well known were the works of Paul Gruel, André Bruel, Jean Lambert, Alfred Latour, Jeanne Langrand, Yseux, Louise Germain, and Germaine Schroeder, whose creations in many instances matched those of their more celebrated colleagues. The new enthusiasm for bookbinding also drew in graphic artists, for example,

Right: A French poster utilizing a similar typeface and geometric design to the book covers of the period.

Maurice Denis, George Barbier, Georges Lepape, and Raphael Drouart. The artist-turned-decorator André Mare incorporated a pair of love birds, in engraved and tinted parchment, for his cover design for *Amour*, commissioned by Baron Robert de Rothschild.

In other Western countries, the finest bookbinders adhered largely to traditional materials, methods, and designs.

BRITAIN AND THE UNITED STATES

However, mass-produced, printed covers in Germany, Britain, the United States, and elsewhere also depicted Art Deco figures and motifs. The stylized lettering which came to be associated with 1920s' Paris was also often seen. A 1932 English-language edition of Bruno Bürgel's *Oola-Boola's Wonder Book* displays such lettering – bold, in several sizes and decorated in blind-stamping with simple vertical and horizontal bands.

In the United States, the Greek-born John Vassos and Ruth Vassos designed and produced bindings of note, often for their own, colored-cloth-on-board books, which included *Contempo* (1928), *Ultimo* (1930), and *Phobia* (1931). These catchy, contemporary titles appeared in thick, bold lettering on grounds highlighted by equally bold geometric designs. Vassos was also known for his industrial designs. The American-born Edward McKnight Kauffer, then working in Britain, was the designer responsible for the book jacket for H. G. Wells's *The Shape of Things to Come* (1935).

The book and fashion-magazine illustrators of the 1910 to 1914 period anticipated the later Art Deco graphic style. Inspired primarily by the 1909 arrival in Paris of the Ballets Russes and Léon Bakst's vivid stage and costume

L'Asie

Left: This lovely illustration by the British graphic artist and illustrator John Austen adorned the frontispiece of a 1928 limited-edition of 500 copies of Manon Lescaut.

Far left: The delicate ornament and costume of Asia, as reinterpreted in Art Deco style by George Barbier, 1920.

ANTINÉA

Manteau du soir, de Paul Poiret

designs, French commercial artists followed suit, introducing an orgy of colors and medley of Persian, Oriental, and Russian influences into their designs for book illustrations, fashion plates and theater sets. Couturiers such as Paul Poiret provided additional opportunities in the same style for such employees as Erté and Paul Iribe, by publishing volumes of their newest fashions.

FASHION ILLUSTRATORS

By the time of the outbreak of World War I, Bakst-inspired *pochoirs* and aquatints dominated the pages of Paris's foremost fashion magazines, *La Gazette du Bon Ton, L'Illustration,* and *La Vie Parisienne.* The first mentioned in particular drew on the talents of a host of artists, including George Barbier, Edouard Garcia Benito, Georges Lepape, Robert Bonfils, Umberto Brunelleschi, Charles Martin, André Marty, Bernard Boutet de Monvel, and Pierre Brissaud. These artists mixed eighteenth-century pierrots, columbines, powdered wigs, and crinolines with women clad in the latest *haute-monde* creations. From 1920, the lightly sensual young woman of these transitional years was transformed into a chic *garçonne* (girl-boy), a willful coquette who indulged in sport and cigarettes.

ERTÉ

Of these illustrators, the Russian émigré Erté (born Romain de Tirtoff) gained lasting fame as a designer – first in Paris and later in the United States. Not only did he create minutely detailed fashion plates from 1913 until after World War II, but he was still working at the

Left: A fashion plate created by Georges Lepape which appeared in La Gazette du Bon Ton *in 1920.*

Left: A highly stylised holiday greeting card dating from c.1925 signed by the artist Renbal.

time of the Art Deco revival during the 1960s. Between 1924 and 1937 he was exclusively contracted to design covers and illustrations for *Harper's Bazaar*. Working in a manner closely allied to Parisian Art Deco, Erté did much to convey a fashionable European sophistication among other American magazines, a highly desirable ability when Europe was in vogue as *the* fashionable place. Erté also worked in other disciplines, thus continuing the penchant for the multimedia designer. Consequently, the success of his stage sets, fabric designs, and graphics meant that he attained unparalleled status on two continents as a designer with his finger on the pulse of European-inspired *Art Moderne*.

GERMAN ILLUSTRATORS
Elsewhere in Europe, the response to the French Art Deco style was sporadic and mixed. In Germany, the fashion revue *Die Dame* followed the lead of its French counterparts, as did the German-born illustrator Baron Hans Henning Voigt, who worked under the pseudonym Alastair, creating haunting images that were inspired by Edgar Allan Poe. Alastair spent most of his career in England before moving to the United States.

AMERICAN FASHION MAGAZINES
The French Art Deco graphic style reached the United States during the late 1920s, where it quickly evolved into a Modernist idiom in which the machine's influence was increasingly felt. Fashion magazines such as *Vogue* and *Vanity Fair*, *Harper's Bazaar*, and *Woman's*

Left: A 1939 watercolor of a stylish interior by André Edouard Marty, whose illustrations often appeared in the Gazette du Bon Ton.

Above: William Welsh's cover for the February 1931 issue of the American magazine, Woman's Home Companion.

Left: Erté's exotic costume design for the character of Assad in the ballet Dance de Jouet *from* A Thousand and One Nights.

Left: This 1920s' advertisement illustrates the Art Deco preference for sans-serif typefaces and geometric motifs.

Home Companion included French-inspired stylizations in their advertisements. To impress their readers, editors invited such European illustrators as Erté, Benito, and Lepape to contribute cover designs. Other periodicals, such as *The New Yorker* and *Fortune*, tended toward a more geometric and industrial style, especially for their covers.

THE EUROPEAN INFLUENCE

Once settled in the United States, European designers found their voices in the pages of the fashion magazines. Notable among them was the Russian-born poster designer Alexey Brodovitch, who had been working in Paris but was the art director at *Harper's Bazaar* from 1934. He employed the likes of Salvador Dalí, Man Ray, and Henri Cartier-Bresson to provide photographs and, with consummate skill, fundamentally altered the rules governing the way in which magazines were to look.

AMERICAN MODERNISTS

Other noted Modernist designers working in the United States during the 1920s and 1930s included Joseph Binder and Vladimir V. Bobritsky – both European expatriates – and the native-born William Welsh, John Held, Jr., and George Bolin. During the 1920s, Rockwell Kent pursued a light Art Deco graphic style in his woodcuts for book illustrations, while John Vassos, the country's premier Modernist in book design, imparted a powerful linearism to his covers and illustrations.